TRINITY COLLEGE DUBLIN
A WALKING GUIDE

Fergus Mulligan

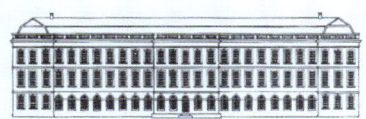

Trinity College Library Dublin

First published in 2010 by
Trinity College Library
Dublin 2
Ireland
www.tcd.ie/library/shop
Tel. +353 1 896 1000

Text © Fergus Mulligan

Unless otherwise indicated all photographs are by John Jordan and © the Board of Trinity College Dublin

Design and printing: Genprint (Ireland) Ltd

ISBN: 978-1-8714-0853-9

All rights reserved. No part of this publication may be copied, reproduced or transmitted in any form or by any means, without the permission of the author and the Board of Trinity College Dublin.

Contents

Foreword by the Provost, Dr John Hegarty 5

Introduction 7

How to use this Guide 9

A short history of Trinity College Dublin 10

Walk 1
Parliament Square to the Museum Building 13

Walk 2
Parliament Square to College Park 25

Walk 3
Science City: the East End of College 37

Map of Trinity College .... Endpapers

Foreword by the Provost, Dr John Hegarty

I would like to welcome you to Trinity College Dublin, Ireland's leading university and one of the top universities in the world. Over 400 years Trinity College has nurtured some of the world's great minds and today TCD graduates are found in every sphere of achievement and excellence. Our 16,800 students come from every part of Ireland and from 114 different countries.

Trinity College's mission is to provide a liberal learning and research environment which values independence of thought and encourages students to achieve their full potential, while developing skills in questioning, problem solving and communication. We aim to achieve this through excellence in research and teaching in an inclusive College community offering equality of access to all for the benefit of Ireland and the international community.

If you would like to learn more about Trinity College or you are thinking of studying or working here please visit our website **www.tcd.ie**.

I welcome the publication of this Walking Guide which introduces visitors and local people alike to the many aspects of our beautiful College campus in the heart of Dublin. Here you will see fine classical architecture, top of the range arts and science research facilities, the magnificent Book of Kells, as well as our latest building to be completed, the Trinity Long Room Hub. All of these combine to create an exceptional centre of learning for our students and a pleasant place for visitors to relax and spend an hour or two.

« The 1937 Reading Room framed by the Trinity Long Room Hub building.
Photo: Fergus Mulligan.

Introduction

Welcome to Trinity College, the University of Dublin, Ireland's oldest and finest university. Founded over 400 years ago in 1592 and located in the heart of the city of Dublin, Trinity is as famous for its splendid Georgian architecture as for the excellence of its graduates. Among them are writers, scientists, statesmen, poets and leaders in every field of human achievement in Ireland and across the globe.

There is no other university campus in the world as open to the public as Trinity. Thousands of people visit the College each year to view the Book of Kells, the world famous 9th century Christian manuscript. Visitors and locals alike enjoy the calm and serenity of our leafy campus and many would like to know more about this peaceful place. To meet that need this Guide brings you all the key places of interest.

As one of the world's leading universities, Trinity is committed to excellence in teaching, research and innovation, offering its students a wide range of courses in the arts, humanities, sciences, engineering and health sciences leading to a wealth of career opportunities. If you are thinking of coming here to study you will be made very welcome; have a look at www.tcd.ie.

We hope this book will be both a congenial companion and a pleasant memento of your visit.

« Parliament Square.

« The Graduates Memorial Building (GMB) from under the Campanile.

How to use this Guide

Trinity College, the University of Dublin, welcomes visitors from Ireland and from all over the world. The beauty, elegance and sense of history are striking as soon as you enter this oasis of quiet in the very heart of a busy capital city. The College is open to all as a public facility and a park and you are welcome to visit at any reasonable hour.

To help you explore Trinity this Guide divides the campus into three walks, each taking 45 minutes to an hour, depending on your pace and the number of stops you make. Routes are colour coded on the map at the end of this book and coffee stops, cafés and shops are mentioned in the text and on the map. During term time (early October-early May) cafés are open Monday-Friday but less frequently from May-September. However there is a wide choice of eating places in the streets around Trinity College. Lavatories are marked on the map with this symbol.

Walks 1 and 2 start and end in Parliament Square. Walk 3 starts at the Leinster Street pedestrian gate and finishes at Lincoln Place gate. Many of the buildings you will see on Walks 1 and 2 are divided into Houses. The House numbers appear over the doorway and are also marked on the map. Please note numbering may not always be strictly sequential as building programmes have altered the campus over the years. It's unlikely you'll get lost but if you do, just hail a passing student and ask for directions.

Trinity is primarily a place of teaching, learning and research. Over 18,000 people study, teach, and work here, many living on campus. While most areas of College are open to visitors, some buildings such as lecture halls, laboratories, residences and most libraries are not. Please therefore respect notices requesting privacy or indicate that certain buildings are closed to the public.

Student led tours starting from Regent House last 30 minutes and run daily from mid-May to the end of September, other times at weekends only.

One way to see normally inaccessible areas of the College is to attend one of the frequent lectures, meetings, concerts, conferences, exhibitions, plays or recitals held in Trinity and open to the public. Or you can sign up for a part-time extramural course in any one of a host of subjects. For information on all these, go to www.tcd.ie.

Enjoy your visit.

« A statue niche set into the wall of the Printing House.

A Short History of Trinity College Dublin

Trinity College Dublin was founded in 1592 during the reign of Elizabeth I. The charter refers to the "College of the Holy and Undivided Trinity near Dublin" and the queen's name is mentioned to this day during grace at Commons, formal dinner.

The College was built on the site of the Augustinian priory of All Hallows, founded by Dermot MacMurrough, King of Leinster in 1166 and dissolved by Henry VIII in 1538. Training clergymen for the Anglican Church of Ireland was a major function of the new college, the first Provost being Adam Loftus, Archbishop of Dublin who like his four successors was from Cambridge University. It was expected Trinity would expand with several more colleges, as in Oxford and Cambridge but this did not happen and Trinity remains the sole constituent College of the University of Dublin.

Most of the first students were schoolboys who took a four year BA course divided into Junior and Senior Freshman years followed by Junior and Senior Sophister years, just as it is to this day. If intended for holy orders, as most were, they studied for another three years to receive an MA.

A century later the conflict between the Catholic monarch James II and the Protestant William of Orange impacted on Trinity, being an exclusively Protestant college. James set out to reinstate the Catholic church and chose to fight for the throne of England in Ireland. On arrival in Dublin he expelled the remaining students and fellows and made Trinity a barracks, appointing Fr Michael Moore as head of the College in 1689, arguably the first Catholic Provost. James' defeat at the Battle of the Boyne in 1690 restored the status quo to the College and to Ireland. He fled to France in such haste that his abandoned followers named him Seámus a chaca: James the turd.

In the more peaceful years that followed, Trinity acquired many of its lovely classical buildings such as the Library, Dining Hall, Printing House and the fine layout of Parliament Square. The 1800 Act of Union abolished the Irish Houses of Parliament (now the Bank of Ireland College Green) and integrated Ireland into the United Kingdom. One impact was that Trinity's Library is entitled to a copy of every book, magazine, journal or map published in Ireland or Britain.

The 20th century brought many changes to Trinity. Women were first admitted as students in 1904 and when the First World War broke out 3,000 students and staff volunteered of whom 454 lost their lives. As a stronghold of unionism Trinity also had to come to terms with the realities of an independent Irish state. It did so in the 1920s and 30s by largely ignoring political changes. Its isolation was strengthened by the Catholic church's ban on students attending, a ban which only a few felt able to challenge.

Further change came in the 1970s and Trinity now draws its students from all social and religious groups in Ireland and from across the world. It is now one of the leading universities globally and builds on its 400 year old tradition of scholarship to foster independence of thought and excellence in teaching, learning and research.

≈ The interior of the 1937 Reading Room.
» A well attended lecture.

WALK 1
Parliament Square to the Museum Building

This walk takes in some of Trinity's loveliest classical squares and buildings, including the Long Room of the Old Library where the Book of Kells is on view.

« The statue of Edmund Burke viewed through the railings beside Front Gate.

The West Front of Trinity College, the main entrance from College Green, dates from the 1750s and faces what was then the centre of the medieval city: Dublin Castle, High Street and Christ Church. Statues of two famous graduates stand close to Front Gate: Oliver Goldsmith (1728-74), writer and satirist on the right and Edmund Burke (1729-97) on the left. Burke was a noted debater in the Irish House of Commons which once met opposite the entrance to Trinity in what is now the Bank of Ireland.

As you enter College past the porter's lodge, note the octagonal shape of Regent House vestibule reflecting the shape of an overhead dome which was planned but never built.

« The main entrance to Trinity from College Green with the former Irish Houses of Parliament in the background.

↗ The view of Regent House from Parliament Square.

Arriving into Parliament Square is always a delight. The range of buildings form a pleasing whole. Your eye is drawn towards the College Chapel, Public Theatre and past the Campanile to the red brick Rubrics building in the distance. The most sought after student rooms in College are in Parliament Square.

Student clubs and societies take over Parliament Square with their stalls for Freshers' Week every October, each outdoing the next in their zealous attempts to recruit student members.

As you walk through the square listen for harmonious sounds from the School of Music in House 5 on your right, once home to the Dublin University Players. The Campanile straight in front is an iconic symbol of Trinity College, designed by Charles Lanyon in the 1850s it stands close to the site of the 12th century All Hallows priory which Trinity College replaced in 1592. The remains of that priory lie underneath your feet, awaiting excavation. Note the three Greek figures on the Campanile keystones: Demosthenes, Socrates and Homer.

↟ Students from the School of Music.

In 1961 student members of the Climbing Club scaled the 29 metre Campanile as a prank and left a red hat on the cross at the top.

The Campanile has two bells, the older, the Provost's Bell dates from about the 15th century and probably came from the original monastic priory where it may have been used to summon the friars to prayer. The Great Bell from 1742 is rung at Commencements (degree conferrals), before Commons (formal dinner in the Dining Hall) and to mark the death of a College Fellow.

Turn back towards Regent House and note the arched colonnade of the Public Theatre, or Examination Hall to the left matching that of the College Chapel facing it across Parliament Square. Exams and concerts take place in the Public Theatre as well as Commencements, a colourful ceremony held entirely in Latin marking student graduation and conferral with their degree.

↟ The Campanile.

↖ Public Theatre frontage.

The distinctive colours of academic hoods and gowns worn by postgraduate students signify the degree a person is receiving.

One academic estimated in 1991 that in its 400 odd years Trinity has had only 92,000 graduates, a little more than the capacity of Croke Park, the largest sports stadium in Ireland. The figure 20 years on is doubtless higher but even if there were an average of 1,500 graduates per year since then, that gives a total of just over 120,000. Trinity does not hand out degrees lightly.

Less formal than Commencements is the odd boxing match in the Public Theatre and the Trinity book sale each Spring which attracts large numbers of booklovers.

↖ PhD candidates entering the Public Theatre at Commencements.

↖ Robert Redford and John Hume receiving their honorary degrees.

The 1937 Reading Room set back and to the left of the Public Theatre was built originally as the Hall of Honour to commemorate 454 members of College killed in the First World War. One of them, Captain Clement Robertson died at Passchendaele in 1917 and was awarded the Victoria Cross. The Reading Room is now a peaceful postgraduate study centre.

Above the entrance columns is the word NIKH, the Greek goddess of victory and the theme continues with victory garlands around the pediment. Turn right between this building and East Theatre to catch glimpses of the delightfully secluded Provost's Garden on the right. The Provost is the head of the University, appointed for 10 years and lives in a magnificent house which you can just glimpse on the far side of the garden. The Provost has a most respectable address: No.1 Grafton Street.

Straight in front is Trinity's newest building, the Trinity Long Room Hub, designed by McCullough Mulvin architects and open in September 2010. It is the University's Arts and Humanities Research Institute and acts as a springboard for advanced research. The four storey granite clad building stands over the Edmund Burke Theatre and faces onto Fellows Square. It also displays some of the Library's treasures and provides additional research and lecture rooms. It may look a little severe but will doubtless settle into its new home in time.

≈ Trinity Long Room Hub, the most recent building on the campus to be completed. Photo: Fergus Mulligan.

Walk round the 1937 Reading Room to pass the Trinity Long Room Hub on your right and as you enter Fellows Square turn right and walk up the ramp leading to the Arts and Social Sciences building of 1978, designed by Paul Koralek. Inside to the left and down the stairs (there's also a lift) is a coffee shop serving sandwiches, snacks and drinks, should you need refreshment. Straight ahead on the right going towards Nassau Street is Trinity's own art gallery, the Douglas Hyde Gallery. Hyde was a Trinity graduate and a noted Gaelic scholar who became President of Ireland. Specialising in exhibitions of Irish and international contemporary art, the Gallery is open to the public and entry is free. Further information from www.douglashydegallery.com

Continue on as if heading towards Nassau Street and just before you reach four shallow steps look through the railings to the right. Underneath where you are standing is what is believed to have been St Patrick's holy well, an ancient place of pilgrimage which gave its name to the adjacent Nassau Street once called St Patrick's Lane.

Retrace your steps back to Fellows Square and at the top of the ramp admire the splendid lines of the Old Library opposite, built by Thomas Burgh in the early 1700s. Thousands of visitors come here to see the Book of Kells, a beautifully decorated manuscript of the four gospels created by 9th century monks and one of Ireland's most precious treasures.

Old Library and Book of Kells Opening Hours:

The Old Library is open Monday to Saturday from 09.30 to 17.00, Sundays May-September from 09.30 to 16.30 and Sundays October to April from 12.00 to 16.30

↑ Arts building and Fellows Square.

↟ Ussher Library pyramid.

Among the other treasures on display is an ancient Irish harp, said to have belonged to Brian Boru. This harp is the model for the national symbol for Ireland. Guinness also uses a version of this harp and in return the brewery provides a free glass of stout to each College diner on Commons.

The Long Room is one of the loveliest rooms in Europe with shelves of books running on two floors right up to the beautiful vaulted ceiling. Not to be missed. The Library Shop here has an excellent selection of books, crafts and souvenirs of your visit to Trinity College.

In the middle of Fellows Square is a metal sculpture, *Cactus* by Alexander Calder while the stepped frontage of the Arts and Social Sciences block is in sharp contrast to the straight lines of the Old Library facing it. At the east end of Fellows Square is the Berkeley Library, also designed by Koralek and named after Bishop George Berkeley, (1685-1753). He was a famed Trinity philosopher and psychologist whose ideas influenced Hume and Kant and who gave his name to the University of California, Berkeley.

↟ *Cactus*, in Fellows Square.

Walk up the concrete steps to the right between the Berkeley Library and the Arts Building leading up to a small piazza overlooking College Park. Straight in front are the rather severe exterior lines and gun-slot like openings of the Ussher Library, named after Archbishop James Ussher (1581-1656), who donated his large book collection to the infant College library. He is famous for dating the creation of the world to 23 October 4004 BC precisely. Through the Ussher Library windows you can glimpse students at work and a nearby study room is open 24 hours a day for insomniacs or night owls.

At the opposite side of the piazza to the one you entered are glass doors through which you can see the light-filled interior of the Ussher, comprising three prismatic blocks on a podium. Directly opposite from where you entered the piazza, with the elongated glass pyramid on your left, take the narrow passageway leading towards the Nassau Street railings. This brings you to a second piazza with a matching pyramid, this one in stone. From here take the ramped zig-zag incline down to College Park and at the end note the large tree on the right close to the wall. Behind it set in the wall is a plaque to a British soldier, Charles Arthur Smith, killed nearby during the 1916 Easter Rising. Trinity being staunchly unionist then, took the British side in the conflict.

↑ The steps leading up to the piazza linking the Berkeley and Ussher Libraries.

The officers and cadets of the former University Officer Training Corps erected the plaque and the 4th Hussars Association restored it in 2007. Notice the drop of several metres from street to ground level indicating the antiquity of the campus.

Turn around and walk towards the Museum Building, with College Park on

↑ Cricket in progress in College Park.

Building now on your left. As you walk along note the roundels, arched windows and tall, slender chimneys conveying the air of a rather lavish Venetian palazzo.

At the end of the Museum Building turn left through a set of arched metal gates and linger for a while in the pleasant little garden on the right designed by Lanning Roper. Benches commemorate distinguished members of College and their families. Note the sundial set into the end wall of House 40 facing into the garden, honouring David Webb, former Professor of Botany.

your right and you may see a game of cricket or races in progress, depending on the time of year.

Pause at the start of the short ramp where the corner of the Berkeley Library meets the Museum Building. This is an architectural junction par excellence showing how Trinity's building stock has been added to successfully over the centuries. Within view left to right are the 20th century Berkeley Library, a corner of the Old Library and the end of the Rubrics building both dating from the 1700s and the 19th century Museum Building designed by Thomas Deane and Benjamin Woodward. With the ramp behind you and College Park to the right, follow the line of the Museum

↑ A corner of the Museum Building.

⌃ The Museum Building, built in the style of a Venetian palazzo.

Continue around the two sides of the Museum Building with pleasant views of New Square on your right. Note the fine solid doors at the entrance to the Museum Building with the arms of the University of Dublin above the doorway. At the end of the square, a podium opens up on the left connecting three College squares. Go up the steps to admire Arnoldo Pomodoro's striking sculpture at the entrance to the Berkeley Library, *Sphere within a Sphere*. Looking right along the Old Library you can see the pretty octagonal lantern window above the 1937 Reading Room, now somewhat dominated by the Trinity Long Room Hub building. Go back down the steps and turn left past the end of the Rubrics into Library Square and walk along the north arches of the Old Library. At one time these arches were open to the elements and with the River Liffey running nearby, the book stock was kept on the first floor to protect it from flooding.

When you go past the corner of the Old Library you are once more into Parliament Square with Regent House straight in front. If a refreshing cup of tea, coffee or a tasty lunch beckons head for the Buttery, to the right of the Dining Hall.

« The entrance to the Museum Building with the arms of the University of Dublin set above the doorway.

WALK 2
Parliament Square to College Park

This walk covers the northern half of the campus and brings us to some of Trinity's most delightful buildings, among them the College Chapel and the Dining Hall.

We start at Parliament Square on the College side of Regent House. Turn immediately left and follow the line of houses as far as House 10, until you come to the colonnaded entrance to the College Chapel. This was completed in 1775 to a design by William Chambers who also designed the delightful Casino for Lord Charlemont at Marino in north Dublin, one of the most beautiful buildings in Ireland.

All Christian denominations use the Chapel for services and many alumni choose to hold their wedding here. Evensong is a delight, held at 5.15 pm on Thursdays during term time and sung by the College Choir. Visitors are welcome but please do not walk around during the service. Note the twisting ironwork supporting the lantern over the entrance porch with both lantern and Corinthian columns matching those

↑ Chapel interior.

in the Public Theatre across the square. Turn left past the Chapel and walk down a narrow passageway till you come to a short flight of steps on the left. This leads to the rather curious Challoner's Corner set at an angle where six

« The Dining Hall.

≈ The Chapel ceiling.

Provosts are buried as well as the distinguished historian and biographer of Parnell, F.S.L. Lyons. Before leaving this shadowy corner note the dank steps which disappear eerily down to the Chapel crypt.

Retrace your steps to Parliament Square and on your left is one of Trinity's very finest buildings, the 18th century Dining Hall. The clock in Trinity blue above the superb flight of steps is similar to the one in Parliament Square. Commons (formal dinner) takes place every weekday evening in termtime. The Latin grace dates from 1627 and is recited from memory by a Trinity scholar.

≈ A group about to take Commons in the Dining Hall.

Scholars are chosen from the most outstanding Senior Freshmen (second year students) who sit a demanding exam and are selected on the basis of their results and their overall contribution to College life. They receive free rooms, Commons and

« Shadows on the Chapel doors.

↑ Students lunching in the Buttery.

tuition for the rest of their time in Trinity along with a modest stipend. Each year on Trinity Monday at the start of Trinity Week which is held in early summer, the Provost announces 10 names from the steps of the Public Theatre. Trinity Week consists of seven days of College Races, parties, exhibitions and special seminars culminating in the Trinity Ball, an all night extravaganza described as the largest private party in Europe. It is a sort of Mardi Gras before the start of the exam season.

To the right of the Dining Hall is the Buttery, much used by students for informal eating, snacks, full meals or just to socialise. Visitors are welcome to use the Buttery. As you leave note how the Long Room Hub across the square forms a neat backdrop like a perforated screen to the 1937 Reading Room.

Turn left into the passageway between the Dining Hall and the Graduates Memorial Building which leads into Botany Bay, containing several tennis courts. Students of every era tend to rename parts of their College, often irreverently, names which in time become official. The name of this square does not derive from botanical activity but allegedly from the prison-like nature of the buildings, mainly student residences. This is rather harsh for today its comfortable rooms make it a peaceful enclave resounding to the regular thwack of tennis balls. Walk clockwise round the square and as you turn the corner at Houses 15 and 14 note the elongated view of the range of stone houses leading to the ruby-red brick of the Rubrics.

At House 27, the College inter-denominational chaplaincy, turn left across a roadway known once as Carter's Alley running down to Pearse St. In front are the Doric columns of the delightful Printing House, dating from the 1730s. This is one of Richard Castle's first major works. He also built Leinster House, Carton House, the Rotunda

≈ Fencing, one of the many active sports clubs in College.

Hospital, Powerscourt House and Westport House. Over the door a plaque in Latin from 1734 thanks the donor who paid for construction of the Printing House, John Stearne, Bishop of Clogher and Trinity Vice-Chancellor. The building has three floors: the gloomy basement for printing machines, the ground floor flooded with light where compositors assembled the metal type and the attic for paper storage. In 1837 Michael Henry Gill was printer to the University in this building, producing many of the College's books. In a neat symmetry his descendant, Michael Gill of Gill & Macmillan, published *The Trinity Year: A Portrait of Trinity College Dublin* in 2009 (see p.48).

The Department of Electronic and Electrical Engineering now uses the Printing House while the basement still has working printing machines for students of art history.

≈ The Printing House.

Our route is now through New Square dating from the mid-1800s, past Houses 33-37 and a thoroughfare known as the Narrows. These houses are mainly for resident academic staff. While teaching in Trinity, Samuel Beckett lived in House 39, once home to Mathematics now the Law School. Pass through the narrow gap between Houses 37 and 38 and on your left is the striking wooden-framed Samuel Beckett Centre, home to Drama and Theatre Studies. Designed by de Blacam and Meagher, it also houses the Players Theatre and the Samuel Beckett Theatre. The Centre stages excellent and innovative student productions throughout the year, the equal of many professional theatre companies and gives drama and English literature students first hand theatre experience.

Productions are open to the public, for an events programme see www.tcd.ie/Drama/samuel-beckett-theatre or phone 01 896 2461

Continue on towards the rugby ground on the right, once scrubland called the Wilderness where snipe were shot for high table. In 1899 a hurricane cleared this scrubland and the rugby men quickly claimed ownership. Among the Irish rugby internationals who cut their teeth on the Trinity ground are Philip Orr, Hugo MacNeill, John Robbie and Brendan Mullin. Continue east and if it is a nice day you may hear the sounds of little people chattering and playing in the College crèche nearby.

Notice the narrow strip of raised ground running alongside the north side of the

⌃ Drama students.

rugby pitch on your right. This is deliberately left uncultivated and natural to encourage wild grasses as part of ecology studies. Go past the low red brick civil engineering building designed by Thomas Drew and the greatly expanded Simon Perry building next door (we cover the science buildings you can see straight in front on Walk 3). Continue round the rugby ground bringing you to a pleasant tree-lined walk with the pitch on the right and College Park on the left. Just before the Museum Building turn right through the gates, then left along two sides of New Square. Before you reach the Printing House turn left between Houses 26 and 27 to Library Square and walk along the front of the red-brick Rubrics building, Houses 22-26.

The Rubrics are the oldest surviving buildings in College, dating from about 1700, with each house number in latin numerals set in a stone lintel over the entrance door. At one time the Rubrics was directly connected to a range of buildings known as Rotten Row whose name may derive from prevalent odours nearby or just an uncomfortable building. It was demolished in the late 1890s to make way for the Graduates Memorial Building (the GMB) which is now behind you.

↟ Doorway to house XXIV (24) in the Rubrics.

The distinguished writer John McGahern had rooms in House 25 as Trinity Writer Fellow. Plumbing was very basic in those days with the bathroom some distance away from the house. A colleague suggested an alternative to him: "My solution to the problem is to keep a large, flowery teapot in my room. It looks very well – people often admire it – but I never use it for making tea."

This corner of the Rubrics has another claim to fame, or rather notoriety, being the scene of an academic homicide 276 years ago. One night in March 1734 a group of students were partying noisily and came up to the rooms of a less than popular Fellow, Edward Forde, who lived in House 25. The students smashed the windows of his rooms and shouted abuse at the College member. In a rage Forde seized his pistol and despite the efforts of a colleague to restrain him, fired at his tormentors. A shot came from below and Forde fell back, mortally wounded. In line with best medical practice of the time, a surgeon attempted to bleed him, adding to the poor man's suffering; he died soon after. Four students went on trial for murder but were eventually acquitted and although

The Rubrics, scene of a murder most foul.

≈ Croquet in New Square.

Trinity expelled them, all went on to enjoy successful careers. Eminent historian R.B. McDowell observed that Trinity in 1730 had its share of high-spirited, extravagant and wild young men.

Oliver Goldsmith lived in House 22 on the south-east corner. His statue stands in front of Regent House and he is famous for his satirical poem *The Deserted Village* and plays such as *She Stoops to Conquer*.

At one time there was a proposal to build a Bridge of Sighs to connect the Rubrics to the Old Library, a pleasant notion.

≈ A passageway near the Rubrics.

Turn back to House 24 and take the path through the centre of Library Square leading to the Campanile. This path opening is marked by elaborate scrolled railing supports. On either side of the lawns admire the Oregon maples which date from the mid-1800s. To the right there is a fine view of the Graduates' Memorial Building largely funded by graduates to commemorate Trinity's 300th anniversary in 1892 with a building similar in purpose to the Union at Oxford and Cambridge. Designed by Thomas Drew the GMB opened in 1902 and contains the meeting rooms of the Philosophical Society (the "Phil") founded in 1684 and the Historical Society (the "Hist") founded in 1770 as well as student rooms. Further on to the right is the Henry Moore piece *Reclining Connected Forms*.

Walk under the Campanile and just beyond it note the seated figures on either side. One is Provost George Salmon, mathematician and theologian while the other is noted historian Edward Lecky who gave his name to one of the College libraries.

Continue straight ahead to Parliament Square, where this walk began, calling in if desired to the Buttery beside the Dining Hall or the Students' Union shop in House 6 just to the right of Front Arch for a refreshing cool drink, a snack or for a Trinity scarf, sweatshirt or tie. The SU also runs an excellent co-operative second hand bookshop on the second floor.

↑ The Campanile with the Dining Hall.

« The Rubrics at night.

WALK 3
Science City – the East End of College

This walk takes in the lesser known science quarter of Trinity with some superb recent buildings located in an area few visitors see.

Most of the science and health science schools are at the east end of College, an area which attracts fewer visitors than other parts of the Trinity campus. This is a pity because while it may not have the fine classical buildings of the west end there is a lot going on here in an exciting modern environment. Trinity researchers are busy tackling universal health problems such as a cure for cancer, immune system malfunction, the cause of brain diseases and whether excessive cleaning causes allergies. The world's first nicotine patch, for example, was developed in the labs of Trinity's Science City.

Our walk starts at the Leinster Street pedestrian entrance to Trinity or you can set out from Parliament Square, allowing an extra 4 minutes to reach our starting point. (If the Leinster Street gate is closed walk round past the Dental Hospital to

⇖ Finns Hotel.

the Lincoln Place gate and inside Trinity follow the road back towards the Parsons Building described below). Before entering College note the tall red brick building on the right with the faded but still legible sign on the brickwork for Finn's Hotel. Norah Barnacle worked as a chambermaid in this hotel when James Joyce met and courted her on Bloomsday, 16 June 1904, celebrated in his masterpiece *Ulysses*.

Inside the gate go up the short flight of steps and turn right onto a small piazza, Parson's Podium. The Parsons Building houses the Department of Mechanical and Manufacturing Engineering and is named after the distinguished 19th century Irish engineer Charles Parsons who invented the first steam turbine generator. The podium leads into the rear of the curved buildings of Lincoln Place. Straight in front an elaborate sculpture is visible through the windows of the new section of the University Dental Hospital which was designed by Ahrends Burton and Koralek

Go back to the steps and take the flight in front leading down to the Y-shaped Moyne Institute of Microbiology on your left. Designed by Desmond Fitzgerald, it is the gift of the Marchioness of Normanby in memory of her father, Lord Moyne. Alongside is the Pavilion by Thomas Drew which opened in 1885 and is now a popular student bar overlooking College Park.

Ahead and to the right is the Chemistry School and Medical School building on the site of the College's 1750s bowling green and set back past it is the Anatomy

⌃ The Parsons Building.

⌃ Students relaxing in College Park.

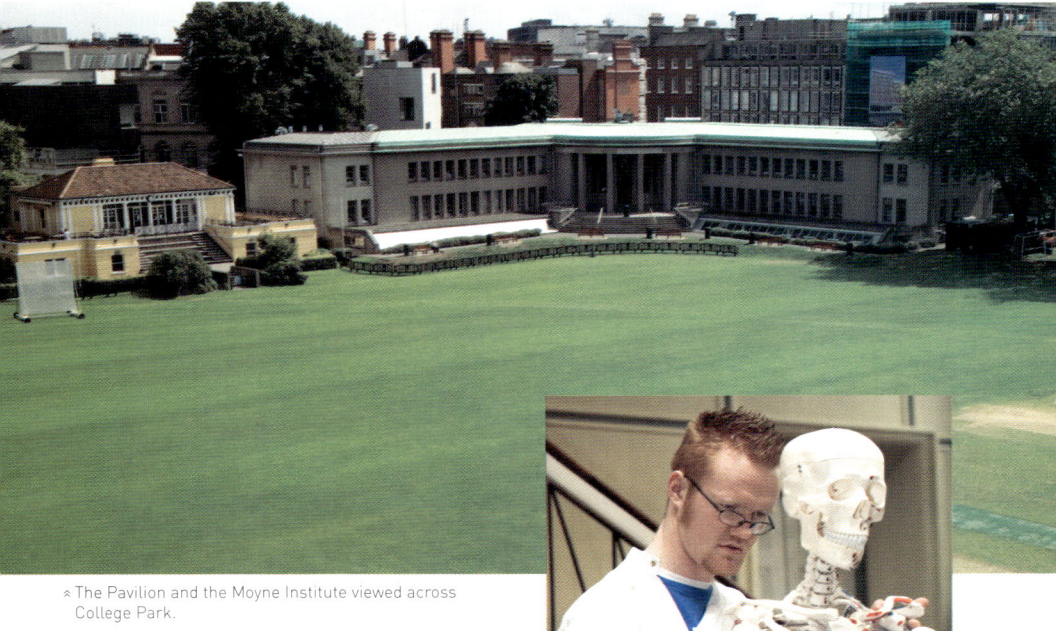

↑ The Pavilion and the Moyne Institute viewed across College Park.

↑ The School of Anatomy dates back to 1711.

Building. Trinity's first anatomy school opened in 1711 in a necessarily remote part of the campus. Many people today donate their remains to Trinity College allowing health science students to conduct investigative work on human cadavers. Trinity keeps a book of remembrance and holds a regular service of thanksgiving for these donors.

Next door to Anatomy is the long frontage of the rather severe Zoology and Physiology building, puritan in its lack of decoration. It was once the College Museum. Zoology has a small fascinating museum of unusual specimens which can be viewed by appointment via www.naturalscience.tcd.ie or phone 01 896 1679.

In front of Zoology is a small pleasant park with benches round the side. Near here was the site of the 18th century bath house "for the use of the gentlemen of the University". Between this small patch of green and College Park is a triangular piece of ground which was the proposed site for a separate Catholic church until common sense dictated shared use of the College Chapel by all denominations.

Straight ahead is the Fitzgerald Building named after distinguished theoretical physicist, George Francis Fitzgerald (1851-1901). He is famous for his 1895 attempted flight when he launched a glider from a ramp down the front of the Pavilion but sadly failed to soar into the air over College Park. A wall plaque commemorates another great scientist, Ernest Walton who won the Nobel Medal with a group of Cambridge physicists in 1932 for their work in splitting the atom.

Walk around the Fitzgerald Building and take the narrow passageway under a glass-sided footbridge between it and the SNIAMS building (Sami Nas'r Institute of Advanced Materials Science). Turn left in front of the pretty Botany Building, designed by Marshall in 1906 with its luxuriant verdant growth all round the front, spoiled somewhat by ugly prefab buildings nearby. Note the elaborate cast iron hopper at the top of each of the drainpipes which appear all round the building, each hopper prominently dated 1907. Proceed towards the rugby ground and then turn right, bringing you to the east end of the Civil Engineering building seen on Walk 2. Turn right here to go around Botany and on the left is the cube-like Luce Building, named after senior fellows and accomplished College sportsmen, A.A. Luce and J.V. Luce. It houses squash courts and a boxing arena.

As soon as you pass Luce Hall the upper section of the striking Naughton Institute building comes into view on the left above the Arches. Continue straight on and turn left under the railway and through an arch to reach the Science Gallery in the Naughton Institute building. This amazing gallery has regular hands-on exhibitions which aim to make science accessible to all. It's also a pleasant place to stop for a coffee or a bite of lunch. For news of exhibitions see www.sciencegallery.com or phone 01 896 4091.

» The ship-like prow of the Naughton Institute. Its ingenious design fits well into a curved space between the railway and Pearse Street.

« The Physiology building.

∧ The Sports Centre with footbridge leading to Goldsmith Hall student residences.

Next door is the excellently equipped Sports Centre open to students, staff and alumni; its sheer climbing wall is best viewed from outside College near the entrance to Pearse Station.

Walk back under the railway arch and turn left at the O'Reilly Institute for Communications and Technology so that the Lloyd Institute containing the Institute of Neuroscience is on your right. Note the 1930s style figures set into the portals of the Lloyd Institute, one featuring the planets and the stars, the other animals and birds. Turn right at the corner of the Lloyd Institute and then right again into a rather narrow

» A Science Gallery exhibition, "Pills", featured a dress made from the contraceptive pill.

» Looking towards the Sports Centre and the Naughton Institute with the Lloyd Institute to the left.

passageway between the latter building and the SNIAMS building. Set into the ground half way along is a pleasing 2-tone pattern known as Penrose tiling. This consists of various shapes including a diamond, five pointed stars, a "boat" and three pentagons. Oxford mathematical physicist, Sir Roger Penrose who researched the aesthetics of pentagons, cosmology and relativity, devised this attractive pattern. This north facing passageway gets little light and few visitors but is well worth a look. The ground and first floors of the Science Gallery have other examples of this tiling.

Go back to the corner of the Lloyd Institute with the steps of the Hamilton Building straight in front. This is named after William Rowan Hamilton, a world class mathematician who graduated from Trinity in 1827. He discovered quaternion equations while walking into College along the Royal Canal and scratched the formulae into the stonework of a bridge, lest he forget it. A plaque near Broombridge marks the spot. NASA used his work on cone-theory during the Apollo 11 programme when calculating the spacecraft's return trajectory from the moon. Quaternions are also used today in satnav devices.

» A detail of Penrose tiling from the ground floor of the Science Gallery. Photo: Fergus Mulligan.

Walk up these steps and before the main door of the Hamilton Building look through the large windows on the left to see an enormous banana tree. Ireland's climate does not really suit banana trees but this one thrives among the mathematicians, evident from the bunches of bananas and giant leaves visible through the windows.

Back down the steps brings you to the area called the Parade Ground, once the Vice-Provost's garden. In the 1940s scientists working here to find a cure for tuberculosis discovered one for leprosy instead which is still saving lives today. Facing the steps, the four buildings to the right, Hamilton, Biotechnology, Pharmacy and Smurfit and the O'Reilly Institute to the left, form a continuous range running from Pearse Street to the Lincoln Gate. When Trinity acquired all the houses on the west side of Westland Row they were in poor condition. Architects Scott Tallon Walker designed a delightful and practical interior streetscape parallel to the outer street to connect all five buildings.

▲ Interior streetscape which runs parallel to Westland Row.

« The sheer face of the climbing wall in the Sports Centre.

↑ A botany lecture in progress.

The best way to view this range is from Lincoln Place.

As you walk under the long colonnade in front of these five buildings, note the view of a sculpture in the far distance, framed neatly as if at the end of a tunnel. This is Brian King's beautiful piece, *Double Helix* and celebrates the 50th anniversary of the discovery of DNA. It stands outside the Smurfit Institute of Genetics.

Through the window in the corner of this building is a bust of Oscar Wilde, the great wit and dramatist. He was born at 21 Westland Row, later moving to the corner of Merrion Square, now the American College in Dublin. The bust celebrates the foundation by his father, Dr William Wilde, of St Mark's Hospital on this spot in 1844. Oscar Wilde studied classics for three years in Trinity but in 1874 moved to Oxford. Gordon Davies relates that his tutor, John Pentland Mahaffy, later Provost, was not impressed at Wilde's defection and advised him: "Go to Oxford, my dear Oscar, we are all much too clever for you over here." A *bon mot* worthy of Wilde himself.

Our walk ends at the Lincoln Gate near where we started. If you feel like a coffee or some lunch head back to the café in the Hamilton Building which is open during term time or to one of the many eateries in the Nassau Street area.

« *Double Helix* by Brian King celebrates the 50th anniversary of the discovery of DNA.

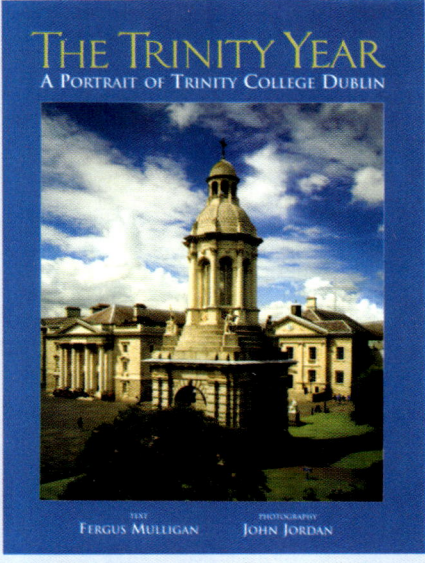

Available NOW from the Library Shop in Trinity and all good bookshops

THE TRINITY YEAR:
A Portrait of Trinity College Dublin

Fergus Mulligan, photographs by John Jordan

The Trinity Year is a celebration of a year in the life of Ireland's oldest and most distinguished university in words and pictures.

With privileged access to all areas the emphasis throughout is on the unexpected, the unusual, the unseen and the surprising with lively, informative text and superb original photography.

This stunning full colour book presents a fully rounded and spontaneous picture of College life that will appeal to visitors, students, alumni and anyone who has ever passed through Front Gate.

Gill and Macmillan, 200 pages, hardback, €40

TRINITY COLLEGE DUBLIN

WALKING MAP